Y0-ARB-427

In the Image of God

A Guide to Sex-Education for Parents

By Sean O'Reilly, M.D.

ST. PAUL EDITIONS

NIHIL OBSTAT
Rev. Richard V. Lawlor, S.J.
Censor

IMPRIMATUR
✠Humberto Cardinal Medeiros
Archbishop of Boston

Cover photo: Sandra Pace

Printed in the U.S.A. by the Daughters of St. Paul
50 St. Paul's Ave., Boston, MA 02130

The Daughters of St. Paul are an international congregation of religious women serving the Church with the communications media.

Contents

ACKNOWLEDGEMENTS

I wish to express my appreciation and gratitude to His Eminence, Patrick Cardinal O'Boyle, for encouraging the preparation of this parental instruction program, and to Monsignor Eugene Kevane for publishing the first edition. The latter is also responsible for stimulating the revised edition and promoting its publication by the Daughters of St. Paul. To them a special word of gratitude is due. Finally, I must thank our youngest daughter, Catherine Grace, for typing the manuscript willingly and expeditiously.

Foreword to the Second Edition

Since the publication of this booklet in 1974, a number of factors have combined to indicate the advisability of a new edition.

A steady demand for copies has continued after the first edition was sold out, suggesting that the need for some such parental guide remains. The relentless pressure to introduce comprehensive detailed sex-instruction programs into the schools has also continued unabated. This is all the more remarkable in the light of the incontrovertible evidence that such programs are harmful to children and rejected by informed conscientious parents. Trenchant criticisms of classroom sex-initiation and behavior-modification programs have continued to appear in various quarters. Two such notable critiques were the articles, "Turning Children into Sex Experts," by Professor Jacqueline Kasun,[1] and "The Betrayal of Youth," by Dr. Rhoda Lorand.[2]

In 1981 a document was published under the aegis of the U.S.C.C. entitled "Education in Human Sexuality for Christians." Its stated purpose was to provide guidelines for a school curriculum of sexual education from pre-school years through high school.

A balanced and careful analysis made by the Religious Education Committee of the Fellowship of Catholic Scholars[3] indicated that the document was "deficient as a guide for sex-education of young Catholics and may be harmful to their formation."

The National Federation of Catholic Physicians Guilds adopted a position paper at their annual meeting in September, 1981.[4] In this paper the physicians came out against the classroom approach and in favor of parental instruction.

Father Henry Sattler, C.SS.R., professor at the University of Scranton and a man with extensive experience in the religious and moral formation of students in the authentic Catholic mode made a separate detailed critique of the U.S.C.C. guidelines.[5] He recommended that they be totally re-written "with adequate consultation with a more inclusive group...*all committed to the constant teaching of the Catholic Church.*"

One of the constant magisterial teachings of the Church has been the insistence on the inalienable right and duty of parents in the religious and moral education of their children, including sexual instruction.

Pope John Paul II recently provided a strong and unambiguous reaffirmation of that teaching in his Apostolic Exhortation on the Family.[6]

Herein is found the final and conclusive argument justifying the timeliness of a revised edition of this guide to sex-education for parents. No substantive revision either of content or format was considered necessary by the author, in the light of current or past magisterial teachings. The final judgment on this matter, however, remains as always with the competent ecclesiastical authority.

NOTES

1. *The Public Interest,* Spring 1979.

2. *Education Update,* Vol. 3, no. 3. The Heritage Foundation.

3. Available from the Fellowship of Catholic Scholars, St. John's University, Jamaica, New York 11439.

4. Position paper available from the National Federation of Catholic Physicians Guilds, 850 Elm Grove Road, Elm Grove, Wisconsin 53122.

5. C.U.F. Newsletter, Vol. 3, no. 3, Nov. 1981.

6. *Familiaris Consortio,* Apostolic Exhortation on the Family, available from St. Paul Editions.

Preface

This program was developed from the studies and deliberations of a group of parents and others whose professional qualifications and activities are in the field of education, medicine, moral theology, pastoral counseling and the law.

It is inspired by a number of convictions whose origins are to be found in the constant magisterial teachings of the Roman Catholic Church on education and moral formation, in the true philosophy of education, and in the findings and principles of sound psychology.

Among these convictions are the following: that in the matter of religious and moral formation, parents are the primary and indispensable educators; that they can be very effective teachers; that explicit classroom instruction in sexuality is a violation of parental rights and of the child's right to privacy; that it is almost invariably disruptive of normal learning; that in such matters "formation" is vastly more important than mere information; that normally the imparting of correct information at the appropriate time is best handled by the parents on an informal and individual basis; that the Catholic school has a very well-defined role in supplementing and confirming the religious and moral formation of children carried out in the first instance by their parents; and that teachers as well as parents need instruction and help in fulfilling their respective and mutually supportive obligations.

Finally, the program is based on the belief that education in sexuality, personality growth and development, guidance—whatever it may be called—cannot exist in a vacuum, cannot be neutral or value-free. It will either be secular humanist, atheistic, irreligious or anti-religious in thrust, or it will be a religious, a Christian, a Catholic program.

The program presented here is a Catholic program structured according to identifiable stages of human physical, psychological and intellectual development. It is informed by the truths of Divine Revelation, notably those concerning the nature of God and the actions in time of the three Divine Persons.

There are nine lectures or seminars in the program, organized in three sets or sections of three as detailed in the introduction. The latter may be repeated if necessary at the beginning of each set, for the benefit of instructors, parents or teachers who may attend only one of the three lecture series because of the ages of the children entrusted to their care.

Each section is more or less self-contained since the basic religious themes are the same in each, though the content and scope increase at each level.

Hence the series may be used in whole, or in part, as an essential core program in the formation of carefully selected instructors whose mission is the provision of help and guidance, primarily to parents who feel inadequately prepared to fulfill their God-given right and duty toward their own children, but also to those teachers who may be required to provide, on an individual basis, such instruction and formation to some children, because of parental delegation. In general the series may also be useful to teachers so that they may be better able to discern and fulfill their collaborative and supportive role in the religious and moral formation of children.

Finally, the series may be used directly by those parents already well informed and actively fulfilling their obligation as primary educators of their children. A limited reading list, additional to the references cited in the foreword, is provided at the end of the booklet. Some of these publications may be read with profit by the children also and are identified appropriately.

Introduction

Each section consists of three chapters, each of which is a lecture based on the same religious or theological theme. Thus each triplet or section is more or less self-contained and oriented toward parents of children of different ages and at different stages of personality growth and development. The stages in question are known as pre-latency, latency and post-latency. In terms of chronological age they correspond approximately to early childhood, middle childhood and late childhood (puberty and adolescence); in terms of schooling, pre-latency children include kindergarten and grades 1 and 2, latency children will be generally in grades 3 through 6, and post-latency children in grades 7, 8 and high school (9 through 12).

There is no excuse for our not knowing the teaching of the Church on education. The rights and duties of parents, the Church itself, the school and the state were spelled out very clearly in Pope Pius XI's seminal encyclical on *The Christian Education of Youth* in 1929, reiterated in *The Declaration on Christian Education* of Vatican II, with copious references to the encyclical and other papal documents, and most recently by Pope John Paul II in his Apostolic Exhortation on the Family.

I urge you to read and study these documents. For our purposes in this program I will confine myself at this point to one quotation from the Vatican II declaration and a comment on it made by Pope John Paul II in his apostolic exhortation.

"Since parents have conferred life on their children, they have a most solemn obligation to educate their offspring. Hence parents must be acknowledged as the first and foremost educators of their children. *Their role as educators is so decisive that scarcely anything can compensate for their failure in it*" (GE 3).

"The right and duty of parents to give education is essential, since it is connected with the transmission of human life; it is *original* and *primary* with regard to the educational role of others on account of the uniqueness of the loving relationship between parents and children; and it is *irreplaceable* and *inalienable* and therefore *incapable of being entirely delegated to others or usurped by others*" (FC).

What do these teachings mean—practically speaking? Surely they imply that parents *can* teach their children, not only by example and non-verbal communication, but also as *teachers;* that parents *must* teach their children religion and provide them with moral formation; that they must educate themselves, by reading, by programs such as this one, etc., so as to be better instructors of their children; that they cannot shrug off their obligation as teachers of religious and moral values to their children and delegate this exclusively to the school; and that they should reject any classroom instruction that contradicts or subverts their own religious and moral teaching.

There are essential facts that parents need to realize and remember since they are very helpful, indeed indispensable, in their educational role.

1. *Example speaks louder than words:* How other than by example, in most cases, can children learn the real meaning of love (sacrificial love); of thoughtful behavior,

respect for the rights of others, modesty; good physical, moral and intellectual habits; spiritual and religious habits such as prayer, attendance at Mass, reception of the sacraments, etc.? Parental example is surely of prime importance in such matters, and a prime necessity for good parents is frequent examination of conscience on this score.

2. *Children are not miniature adults:* They are more simple, more artless, more trusting, more vulnerable in many ways, much more resilient in other ways, more in need of formation than of information, more dependent even when they appear most independent.

3. Of most things that matter *parents know more than their children.*

4. *Children are not clones or carbon copies:* Each is unique, developing at his or her own pace; therefore, instruction in private matters must be private and individual.

5. *Girls are not boys and vice versa:* They develop at a different pace and must be treated differently.

6. *When young children ask questions,* especially questions relating to sexuality, *they are quite frequently simply seeking reassurance,* not detailed factual information.

7. *Children need and frequently subconsciously demand discipline:* It should be firm, consistent and reasonable, but above all benevolent.

8. *Children's questions, especially those concerning sexuality, must be answered, if they are persistent.* The answers must be factual, truthful and appropriate to the child's age, sex and stage of development. Prudence will sometimes dictate a preliminary answer with the promise of further information when the child is older. Examples would be questions relating to immoral behavior of others such as older children, neighbors, etc. One can

never forget our Lord's warnings about scandal, especially of those little ones so dear to Him.

In this program the basic religious theme of each of the three lectures or chapters in each section is the same. The themes are:

Lecture I: God the Father, Creator, Lawgiver.

Lecture II: God the Son, Incarnate, Redeemer, Savior.

Lecture III: God the Holy Spirit, the Sanctifier.

The fundamental truth of Divine Revelation is that truth about God attainable in no other way, namely, that He is three Persons in one God. The mystery of the Blessed Trinity, the doctrine of the Triune Nature of God, is as Cardinal Newman said the central truth of Christianity. The history of the universe, of this planet earth, of life, of human life, your life and my life, is basically the story of the actions in time of these three Divine Persons. The basic truths of the divine life are just as comprehensible to the mind of the child as they are to the most learned and wise adult, since they are mysteries. Surely this was why our Lord said, "Suffer the little children to come to me, for of such is the kingdom of heaven."

Obviously, the scope and content of the lectures developed around the three themes will increase at each level, and the information to be imparted, suffused with the light of the Triune God, will be different in degree and complexity at each level; but the inescapable fact is that unless everything we know, learn and do is scrutinized in the light of the mystery of the Blessed Trinity it will be useless knowledge, perhaps dangerous knowledge, and our lives and those of our children will be largely meaningless.

PART ONE

Pre-Latency Children

— 1 —

The Supernatural Dimension of Human Growth and Development: God, Father and Creator of All Life

This section of the program is directed to parents of young children—pre-school and perhaps 1st, 2nd, 3rd graders—up to age 8 or 9 years, those children who are in the pre-latency period—early to middle childhood.

You may well ask—what do you mean by pre-latency? What is this latency period?

Briefly and simply it is psychiatric terminology for a phenomenon that is a matter of commonsense observation by parents, and indeed a phenomenon that one can recognize in retrospect as a matter of sometimes conscious personal experience at a rather superficial level. Many of you may recall being very interested in the opposite sex at the age of 5, 6, 7, or 8 years—only to have all this cease for a variable number of years during which one was either studiously involved in avoiding the opposite sex or else engaged in heaping scorn on them or furiously excluding them from participation in the activities of one's self and one's peers.

This variable period when the child has discovered himself or herself and has begun to identify with members of his or her own sex is regarded in the Freudian psycho-analytic theory of psycho-sexual development as a time when sexual curiosity and strivings are dormant or latent, hence the term latency. It is a very important period in normal psycho-sexual development and in the learning process. We will consider it more fully in the 2nd lecture series for parents of children in the latency age group—viz., 8 or 9 years to puberty—since its existence and importance is *the* professional argument against detailed formal sex-instruction of young children whether in the classroom or the home.

The topic is introduced here as a definition, by exclusion if you will, of the stage in psychological and personality development your pre-school and grades 1, 2 and 3 children have arrived at.

We would make a serious mistake in accepting as gospel and sole revelation the Freudian theory of psychosexual development. Many of the observations on which the theory is based are simply commonsense ones: interpretation of these clinical observations is another matter and it would be foolish to accept and swallow the interpretational theory uncritically.

There is for example much merit in the Jungian theory that the drive for power is as important in shaping personality and character, as the sex-drive is in Freudian theory, and evidences of this drive in children from a very early age are just as much a matter of common observation as those subserving the Freudian stages of psychosexual development. Who among you has not witnessed the strivings of the infant and young child to master you, his parent, or his environment?—the temper tantrums; the guileless, shameless effrontery; the guile and craft employed to get his or her way.

But there is more to personality development and character-formation than the mechanics of the process at a purely natural level, whether we subscribe to Freudian or Jungian or any other theory.

As Christian parents, we must take the supernatural perspective. We must view the development of the child, who is our primary responsibility under God, in the light of the truths revealed by that God. Primary among these truths, indeed the fountain from which they all inevitably flow is what He has revealed about Himself, about His own divine life. This is the ineffable mystery of the Trinity—three Persons in one God. Now in a most real sense, the individual human family is a faint reflection of the life of the Blessed Trinity. After all, He made us in His own image and likeness.

The love of husband and wife, if it is real—purified by the virtues of chastity and selflessness, sanctified by the graces of the Sacrament of Matrimony—is a reflection, faint but discernible, of the flaming love existing in the Blessed Trinity from all eternity as the unique Person of the Holy Spirit, uniting the Father with the Divine Word, the second Person, God the Son, who is the perfect and unique expression of the Father. He is also the final complete Revelation in time of the nature of God, and of His divine will toward man, His unique creature.

Because it is a reflection of God's love, marital love is necessarily creative, pro-creative usually, since God's intervention is necessary for the creation of each individual soul; above all it is creative and fruitful, since not all marriages are blessed with physical issue, i.e., children—creative and fruitful of many good works, perhaps adopted children, certainly God-children, and surely fruitful of eternal salvation for the couple so joined. Now salvation is simply our union with God for all eternity, caught up in the contemplation, adoration and love of the triune God who created us, redeemed us from sin and sanctified us.

In this life, no matter what the trials and troubles, what immense satisfaction Catholic parents should get as they contemplate the offspring of their mutual love; for them not only have they made physical existence possible, under God's Providence, but in them, by Baptism, they have the assurance of life of an entirely different order—supernatural life, supernatural grace, the indwelling of the Blessed Trinity. With what diligence and loving care will those parents who so believe, labor to foster the growth of that fragile divine spark within that child! They will surely try to envelop him or her with the best facsimile they can master of the tender but strong paternal love of God.

So, as the child, weaned from exclusive preoccupation with nourishment, begins to appreciate and explore surrounding objects, he or she will encounter a consistent, firm, loving parental discipline that will guide development—physical, mental, moral and spiritual. Such parental love will not indulge every whim; neither will it regard temper-tantrums, when the child doesn't get his or her own way, as anything more than normal frustration at failure to immediately master the environment.

Such love will not be rendered impotent by anger or disgust with the child's preoccupation at a given stage with excretions or body-parts, or regard delay in acquiring sphincter-control and toilet-training as willful and perverse, any more than it regards as perverse, anger, aggression and sibling-rivalry when and if other children are born. Rather it will firmly but gently guide the child toward a realization that he or she is not the center of the universe, toward acquiring good physical habits, toward avoiding dangerous objects, toward sharing with others—brothers and sisters in the first place—and toward the recognition that they all share uniquely in that strong, warm and non-exploitative love that envelops them.

This is the child's first, even if indirect, experience of God. And as the small child emerges from the cocoon of self-contemplation and self-concern, and recognizes, albeit in an infantile way, necessary relations with others —especially dependence on the parents—the concept of God as the all-powerful loving Father and Creator can be introduced naturally and accepted by the child.

In the Catholic family, the word "God" will be as familiar to the small child as "Mama" and "Dada." They are such easy words for the child to utter—Mama, Dada, God. But of course vastly more important than familiarity with the name of God is the gradual awareness of at least some of the attributes of God that dawn on the child—variable in each child and depending more perhaps on non-verbal than on verbal communication.

A mother told of overhearing a conversation about God between her eleven-year-old son and his two youngest sisters—ten years and six years old respectively. The boy, a somewhat dreamy contemplative type, said: "When I was little I thought God must be huge and held the world in His hand like a ball." The youngest, a bright, affectionate, soft-hearted little thing, chipped in with "Yeah! and when I was small I thought that when it rained God was crying!" And the ten-year-old sister, a lively extrovert and leader among her peers, spoke up in matter-of-fact tones and said, "When I was young I thought God must be like my Daddy, except of course he has brown hair!" There you have it: God—infinite, omnipotent, compassionate, like us in all things, sin excepted. "Out of the mouths of babes and sucklings, O God, You have perfected praise."

If and when some questions are forthcoming— "Where did I come from?", "Who made me?", "How *did* God make me?"—they can be answered properly and adequately only in the context of creation history and in the light of the triune life and the actions in time of the Three Divine Persons. "Where did I come from?"—"From God, the Creator of all things." The young child sees without perceiving; even though the child sees its mother make a cake or cookies, the idea that all objects in the environment had to have a maker dawns only very gradually and in piecemeal fashion. It is a conscious realization only at times, aided and abetted by personal experience and by myriad extrinsic inputs. The child has no problem accepting the fact that the toys, the familiar furniture, the house itself—all were made by somebody somewhere—somebody he never saw or knew, but whose existence is taken for granted on the word of parents or other persons, coupled with an innate grasp of the abstraction—"maker." So the concept of an invisible, all-powerful Creator of all things, including the child himself, is readily accepted.

The objection that the small child cannot possibly comprehend this stupendous fact is to beg the question. What adult human being, no matter how educated, well-informed or wise, can fully comprehend it either? For we are so totally immersed in "being" that we simply cannot imagine or grasp the state of non-being. We can reason to the conclusion of the philosophers that there must exist a being who is self-sufficient, uncreated, timeless, eternal, since we cannot rationally invoke an endless series of causes or origins of the beings known to us by our senses or by hearsay. But we would know very little else about God had He not revealed Himself to us in various ways and at various times.

So in answer to the child's questions—"Who is God?" "Who made God?"—we can only recapitulate the story of the creation as recounted in the Bible. And when the child insists "but how did God make *me?*" we can help him or her grasp the difference between living and non-living things.

We cannot expect the child to grasp any but the most elementary notions of the physical nature of matter, the nature and properties of the elements of matter and their subatomic constitution, and the laws by which their reactions are governed. But the child *can* realize that non-living things do not multiply except for being broken down into smaller parts. And the child can and does recognize that living things *do* multiply by producing another of the same kind. The elementary facts of biology are all that can and should be presented: that plants grow and produce flowers, fruits and seeds from which other plants of the same kind can be grown; that animals somehow acquire young animals–kittens, puppies, calves, etc., and that human parents somehow get children. All these phenomena are perceived and soon taken for granted by the small child.

It is sufficient for him to be told that in his own case, as with all children, God gave to parents a special share in His creative activity, the formation of the child's body from two special cells, one from the mother and one from the father which are brought together by a special act of love designed by Him for that very purpose. The child can be then informed that God Himself immediately creates the soul or spirit which makes of him or her a living, growing person. These elementary "facts of life" will necessarily have to be repeated and embellished with more detail as the child grows in awareness and understanding.

— 2 —

The Incarnation of God the Son in Relation to Human Growth and Development: Answers to Further Questions

It is inevitable, in the Catholic home, that sooner or later the small child will ask, "What is God?" He will be very familiar with the name, God, both at home and in school, and will have been told that God is the Creator of all things, a spiritual Being, all-wise and all-powerful, a Being who had no beginning and who is eternal, who made time when He created things—the stars, the sun, the moon, the earth.

He told us all we know about Himself:

1. He spoke to us without words when He gave us the power to see so much that He had made, and the power to reason that He must be immensely wise and all-powerful to have made all these things.

2. He spoke to us through the prophets, those holy men who repeated what He said to the people of Israel; these things were written down in what we call the Scriptures, the Bible. There we find God telling us He is God, that He always will be, that He created all things in the beginning, including our first parents.

3. He told us most about Himself and us when He sent His Son on earth to become man—to be our Lord and Savior Jesus Christ, our Brother, our King.

Despite the repeated effort to recapitulate the essentials of creation and salvation history already covered or being dealt with in religion class, it is perhaps inevitable that the child will come up with the question—"Did God have a father and a mother?"

This is a very opportune question. It provides the occasion for repeating what we know about the nature of God as He has revealed it to us especially through the teachings of our Lord—that God is three Persons in one Being, one Divine Nature—God the Father, God the Son, God the Holy Spirit. How this can be is a mystery—only God Himself can fully understand it. We believe it because He has told us. God had no beginning—therefore he had no father. He is *the* Father, the *Eternal* Father, the First Person of the Blessed Trinity. The Second Person is God the Son, also called the Word because He is the perfect expression of the Father, like Him in all ways, and equal to Him in all ways. The Third Person of the Blessed Trinity, God the Holy Spirit, is the living, loving force personified, that unites all three Persons in the one God.

But God has a Mother. When God sent His Son, the Second Person of the Blessed Trinity, on earth to become man to make reparation for the sin of our first parents, Adam and Eve, and to redeem us—as the child has already learned in the religious instruction class—He had selected Mary, the Blessed Virgin, to be the Mother of His Son, the God-man.

"How did she become His Mother? Was God the Father Mary's husband then?", the young child may ask. "No, He was not," we reply. "How God became man is a very great and wonderful event which we cannot fully understand in this life, and about which we could never have known if He had not told us about it in the Scriptures. What He told us, and what the Church teaches, as you have heard in your religion class, is that God became man through the power of the Holy Spirit. The body of Jesus, the Son of God made man, was formed directly by the Holy Spirit from an egg-cell, that special cell I told you about the other day, which was a cell produced by the Blessed Virgin Mary's body."

How much more the child can assimilate, or how much more need be said is going to vary from one child to another, and more often than not, most children listen for a little while, then appear satisfied, but return to the question at some other time. It is such a fundamental and central doctrine of the Faith that a great deal of time and effort must be expended in helping the child see beyond the necessarily rudimentary and anthropomorphic notions of reality that are proper to this stage of intellectual development.

Even at this stage, children do have the ability to grasp, almost intuitively, the essentials of even so sublime a mystery. After all, this is the time of life in which we have no psychological hang-ups about accepting marvels of all kinds in the most matter-of-fact fashion.

So the child will have no trouble in following and accepting an exposition such as that which follows, whether given in one session or, more likely, spread out over many:

"Most living things, including you and me, are made up of cells. The smallest animals and plants, which are so small that we cannot see them without the help of a microscope, a tool which magnifies things—makes them seem larger than they are; these littlest creatures may consist of only one or a few cells. But your body and mine contain millions upon millions of cells. However, no matter how large we are when full-grown, no matter how large the animal—elephant, whale, dinosaur—every one begins life as a single cell which divides into two; each of these divide again and so on until finally there are millions. Some of these form our fingers and toes, our legs and arms; others our heart, head, brain and so on. You will learn more about how this happens as you grow older; what I want you to remember now is that we all began life as a single cell.

"That single cell was a special cell which was formed in a special place in the body of the mother; it was formed when two different special cells joined together to form the special cell from which our bodies grow, somewhat like a plant grows from a seed. You know what a seed is. You have seen many different kinds of seeds and seen different kinds of plants grow from them.

"Now one of the special cells I spoke of just a moment ago is also called a seed–it comes from the father's body, and joins together with the other special cell which is in the mother's body and which is called an egg-cell or ovum. You know what an egg is. You know that birds lay eggs and from some of them come young birds.

"As I told you, the two special cells, one from the father, the seed, and the one from the mother, the egg-cell, join together to form a new special kind of cell that grows to be a new baby. A new person begins as soon as that extra-special cell is formed, because at that moment God creates a new soul or spirit which He sends into that special cell to make it a new human being, a new person.

"That is how everybody is made–all except one, our Blessed Lord, Jesus. His body was formed in a special way in the body of His Mother, Mary. You see, God is all-powerful. In order to become man he had to have a human body and a human nature. He could have formed a human body from nothing for His Son, just as He created the whole world from nothing. Or He could have let His Son's human body be formed like yours and mine, just as I told you. But He did not. As He told us in the Scriptures, and as the Church teaches us, His body was formed in the body of His Mother Mary in a different way; how, we don't know, except that it was by the power of the Holy Spirit, the Third Person of the Blessed Trinity. Then God the Son took that newly-formed body as His own, so that He, already a divine Person with a divine nature, became a divine Person with two natures—one divine, one human—and after His body had grown big enough to be born, He *was* born—the baby Jesus, in a stable in Bethlehem, on the first Christmas night as you have already learned.

"So you see, God-made-man had no human father. He willed it to be that way, but He had a human Mother, Mary. She was the Mother of the man, Jesus, but since Jesus was also God, she became the Mother of God also.

"But you know that as well as helping the mother to form the body of her baby as I told you, a human father also has the important job of protecting and looking after the mother and baby. And so God gave Jesus a human foster father, St. Joseph. Do you know what a foster parent is? It is a person who adopts as his own a child whose parents have died, or who has been abandoned.

"St. Joseph was pledged to be married to Mary when the archangel Gabriel told her she was to become the Mother of God; we repeat what the angel said to her every time we say the 'Hail Mary.' And St. Joseph did take Mary as his wife though they had no other children and lived like brother and sister rather than as man and wife.

"You will understand more about this later on. In the meantime I want to tell you why God did come on earth in this manner—born like any other baby from a human Mother, Mary, and living and growing up in a family with His Mother and foster father. Why did He come this way, when He could have come as a full-grown man, since He is all-powerful and can do anything?

"One reason was to show us how important the family is and to give us the good example of His own Holy Family, so that we might learn how to live together, love one another and help one another in every way as He and Mary and Joseph did in Nazareth long ago."

— 3 —

The Work of the Holy Spirit in Human Growth and Development

It is difficult indeed to maintain a firm grasp on theological exactitude in attempting to answer as simply and accurately as possible the innocent, inevitable, and artlessly profound questions of small children.

The depth of the mysteries of the Blessed Trinity and the Incarnation is so great, and human language so inadequate to express these truths, that we inevitably flounder about frequently seeking words and analogies that the child can understand.

But it is vital that we do so, and that we turn *ourselves* repeatedly to study and reflection on the teachings of the Church.

For the knowledge we are trying to impart to our children at this stage of their development is of supreme importance in their formation of a correct self-concept, their awareness of their apparent insignificance as individuals in the face of God's stupendous creation, contrasted with their incalculable importance as unique persons created by God—in His eyes so important that He sent His only Son to become man, to redeem *me!* The grasp of this profound paradoxical truth—our utter insignificance in the face of the immensity and majesty of God and His utterly gratuitous and benevolent conferring of such extraordinary significance on us—this is of the utmost importance in development of the virtue of true humility, that virtue which is the fountainhead of all moral virtues, of holiness. Its importance in normal psycho-sexual development and Christian personality growth cannot be overestimated. The facts of revelation, of course, as enshrined in the doctrinal definitions of the Church and expressed in her exact language, speak for themselves and are of enormous help.

Thus when explaining how God became man—in answer to the child's question, "Was God the Father Mary's husband then?"—our answers were dictated by the theological facts: God sent His Son, the Second Person of the Blessed Trinity, on earth to become man; the Son, being also God and of one mind with the Father, freely came. Being omnipotent, He could have come in any way He chose; He chose a particular manner of coming; God the Holy Spirit, the living flame of love proceeding from both Father and Son and uniting all three Persons in the triune Godhead, effected that miraculous manner of becoming a man.

The child will surely want to know why God went to such trouble. The simple and adequate answer is because God loves us. But in the interest of the child's education, and in accordance with his or her capacity to listen and understand, we would do well to take this opportunity to recapitulate the creation story, dwelling on the creation of those unique beings, the angels—their nature as spirits, the mystery of free-will, the revolt of Lucifer and his followers, their expulsion from heaven. Then the story of our first parents; all that God did for them; their disobedience of His command—original sin; its effects; the enormity of sin. And then the astounding fact of God's extraordinary love and clemency:

1. The promise of a redeemer;
2. The story of all God did for the chosen people of Israel;

3. The Incarnation as the fulfillment of God's promise to our first parents.

The details of creation and salvation history will be imparted to your child over the course of many years of religious instruction. What we are concerned about at this stage of the child's development is to ensure that he or she is aware of the elementary facts which are essential to the growth in the child of a realization of the infinite majesty and goodness of God and the enormity of refusing to obey His commands, a sense of the child's own worth in the sight of God, some understanding of the difference between original sin and personal actual sin, and the effect of the former in weakening the will so that the latter (actual sin) is harder to avoid. Analogies, imperfect though they may be, can be helpful here:

For instance, a man born blind, through no personal fault of his own, is so handicapped that he is in danger of bumping into furniture, or falling over objects and hurting himself, even killing himself. The latter event would inevitably cause anguish to his parents, as well as effectively depriving them of his presence and removing him from their love and care. The analogy between this and the actual and potential results of mortal sin is clear. The latter displeases God, removes us in a real way from His presence, and if we die in this state we effectively separate ourselves from Him forever.

If the blind person, at any given time, has no option but to fend for himself and take a chance on injuring himself, then this is justifiable—a clear analogy to necessary occasions of sin. If he foolishly and wantonly endangers himself when there is no need to, when he could get help to find his way about, then he is like the person who needlessly and deliberately puts himself into proximate occasions of sin.

The emphasis throughout in all this attempt at religious and moral formation must be on the love of God and the offense to this loving God that is represented by sin. But hand in hand with this emphasis on doing good and carrying out God's will for us should go a salutary and wholesome fear of the awful consequences of deliberate sin. The fear of God and of the danger of hell seems to be neglected in many catechetical programs nowadays, reflecting no doubt the hedonism and permissiveness of what passes for contemporary culture. But it has ever been part of the Church's pedagogical method, and it is not without interest that behavioral scientists, in their attempted programs of behavior modification and control, are again turning to some system of rewards and punishments, or gains and losses.

It is true that if we loved God enough we would never sin, but it also true that, weakened as we are by original sin, we need the stick of a wholesome and reverential fear as well as the carrot of an eternal reward to help keep us from offending God by sin. We need to instill in the child the conviction that God is *just* as well as good and merciful, that God is not mocked, and that hereafter, if not in this life, the wages of sin is death.

From this death of sin our Lord delivered us by His suffering and death on the cross. The first fruits of that redemption, cleansing from the stain of original sin and restoration of the supernatural life of the soul by sanctifying grace, are applied to each and every one of us by the Sacrament of Baptism.

Since this is the only sacrament the small child has as yet received, it is appropriate and very helpful to refer to it frequently as the marvelous event it was in the life of the child. For it made him or her a child of God as well as being the son or daughter of the father and mother who are so much the focus of the child's attention and love. This turning of the child's attention and affection and trust toward almighty God—this, as it were, spiritual weaning of the child—is vastly more important in his personality development than any mundane concerns such as timely toilet training, oedipal strivings, sibling rivalry, peer rivalry, etc. These things are important also, to be sure, but the child who is receiving the kind of religious and moral formation we have been speaking about in these lectures, is going to have far less difficulty in surmounting the hurdles of normal psycho-sexual development and will become a more wholesome and complete person than could possibly be accomplished by the most diligent application of the principles of psycho-analytic theory and deterministic behavioral psychology.

For our Faith tells us that the work of sanctification is the work of the Holy Spirit, the Third Person of the Blessed Trinity. And sanctification is what personality-development should be all about: "This is the will of God, your sanctification."

And so as your child goes to school, encountering that first and often painful separation from the womb of the home, and as he competes with his peers in the classroom and in games, the character and personality that you have been striving to develop will cope more successfully with these problems of childhood than will that emerging from a home devoid of Catholic life, the life of grace, the personality instead being shaped by hedonism, narcissistic selfishness and permissiveness.

And as your child progresses through his first years of school you can offer him or her no greater help than frequent repetition of the truths of our Faith, the story of our Savior's life on earth, the hidden life of Nazareth no less than His public life, culminating in His redemptive sacrifice of love, the institution of the Church and the sacraments for which you are now helping to prepare your children, those wonderful channels of grace so vital to the preservation of the life of the soul—Penance and the Blessed Eucharist.

These, and the important but ancillary habits of personal and family prayer, are the tools of character and personality development that you are given so that your child may grow and develop into a complete Christian man or woman.

Nothing less than that must be your goal. More than that you cannot do for your child.

PART TWO

Latency Children

— 1 —
God the Father, Creator, Lawgiver

(*Note:* "Latency children" are approximately those in third through sixth grade. It would be well to repeat the points made in the introduction to the entire program even if some of the attendees are parents who listened to Part One.)

What is latency?

In the first lecture of the previous series we promised to consider this question more fully. Those of you who attended that lecture gathered, I hope, that latency, or the latency period, was more or less contemporaneous with middle childhood years, when children are likely to be in grades 3 through 6 in school; these are the pre-pubertal years, 8-12 roughly speaking.

I say "contemporaneous, more or less," rather than "equivalent" because strictly speaking the latency period is not a measure of time or age, but rather a stage in maturation of the child, in what, since Freud, has been called psycho-sexual development.

In order to put the matter in perspective, to understand the meaning of such a term, and the significance of the reality underlying the expression "latency" or "latency period," we must review with you, and try to make intelligible if possible, the concepts and language used in psycho-analytic theory.

Let us grasp the nettle straightaway and say that it is all too easy to be intimidated, even turned off, by the apparently crude and earthy terminology adopted by Freud to explain and identify what he meant by the various stages of psycho-sexual development through which he held every human being must successfully navigate to become a mature, well-adjusted adult person, free of neuroses. We may agree that the language used was somewhat shocking, but we can verify, from observation and experience with our own children, that there are stages in their development, and traits of behavior and emerging character, that correspond roughly with the stages described by Freud.

What are the stages or periods? The first is more or less contemporaneous with infancy, a term used here to indicate a stage of complete dependence on the parents, notably the mother, especially for satisfaction of the instinctual urge for nutritional intake. Hence the term *"oral stage"* is reasonably appropriate.

Elimination of undigested and unabsorbed foodstuffs, and of metabolic wasteproducts, in the stool and urine respectively, are automatic reflex acts regulated by that part of the nervous system known as the autonomic nervous system.

As the child grows older and begins to explore things other than himself, another fundamental drive begins to manifest itself, the aggressive drive, which is also an acquisitive drive, though less narrowly focused than the nutritional one, and directed toward mastery of the environment in the interest of the developing ego.

Included in the environment to be mastered is the mother, with whom conflict is inevitable when her efforts to instill and reinforce acceptable behavior clash with the spontaneous and instinctual drives of the child.

The first overt clash of this sort is frequently centered round the effort at toilet-training; in Freud's day this effort began earlier than it does now perhaps, though there is still in all the so-called advanced societies quite a wide variation in age at which toilet-training is begun. In any event, this stage when some parental efforts at discipline are commencing was called by Freud the *anal stage*.

The third stage, or *genital stage*, so called because it coincides more or less with the time when the child is becoming aware of the difference between father and mother and, in a rudimentary way at least, of the difference between the sexes so far as external genital anatomy is concerned, is a period when in Freudian theory the sexual drive, hitherto satisfied by the close affectionate nutritional relationship with the mother or mother-substitute, is stimulated by the growing awareness and exploration of personal body-parts as well as by the urge to mastery, to acquisition.

In psycho-analytic theory, this stage of development is characterized by childish fantasies and fears related to the mother's increasing attempts at behavioral discipline and the irritation and frustration produced in the child by these attempts, resulting in an ambivalent attitude or mixed feelings toward her. The predominant fear or anxiety is according to the psycho-analysts a castration-complex—in the case of boys, a fear of losing the penis for misbehavior, in the girl a resentment toward the mother because she lacks this organ. In both cases, the resolution of this subconscious anxiety initiates the *Oedipal stage*, or Oedipus complex. This fanciful title, which alludes to the tragedy of Sophocles' hero Oedipus, condemned by the gods to kill his own father and marry his mother, tends to dramatize, if not exaggerate, this stage of personality development when, as a matter of commonsense observation, it is evident that the child is becoming aware of his or her gender, or sexual identity, if you will, and obviously is attracted to the parents of the opposite sex, but sooner or later identifies more or less firmly with the parent of the same sex.

With the satisfactory resolution of the Oedipal conflict the child enters the *latency period* or *latency stage of development*.

The stages of development described above are stages of conflict between the three primary elements involved in intrapsychic dynamics, according to psycho-analytic theory: They are the *id* (the forces and demands of the instinctual, sexual and aggressive drives), the *ego* (the mediating, executive part of the personality which utilizes the uniquely human intellectual language and other capabilities in the task of maintaining an equilibrium while coping with internal and external demands), and the *superego* (the individual's own value system or conscience which embodies concepts of right and wrong, the moral imperatives and ideals). (The definitions of these primary elements are those put forward by the Group for the Advancement of Psychiatry, G.A.P. Report No. 68, Feb. 1968.) We may be repelled or we may be fascinated by the terminology used in psychoanalytic theory of psycho-sexual development.

But most likely you can see, from your experience with your own children of different ages, the validity of the insights (conveyed or intended to be conveyed by the theory) into childish behavior and development. That you or I might choose different terms and language to describe what we have seen or continue to see unfolding before our eyes is not important.

Two things, however, are all important:

First, we cannot simply rest content with psycho-analytic theory, and the permissive, almost detached role prescribed for parents in the upbringing of their children by some schools of psycho-analytic practice.

We know that we teach our children: we teach them well or we teach them ill. We teach them by example and we teach them by precept.

We cannot but help them resolve their conflicts, fears and fantasies and arrive safely in the quiet waters of the latency period if we teach them constantly and consistently, both by precept and by example, that God is our Creator who made us as we are; that He made us as we are for a purpose; that He is the Supreme Lawgiver whose laws are exquisitely designed to fulfill His purpose in creating each individual person; that His purpose for us was initially frustrated by the sin of our first parents, but that as well as Creator and Lawgiver, He is our Father, and is omnipotent, infinite love in Person and in deed. His love, therefore, found a stupendous and uniquely divine solution to the problems introduced into His creation by original sin.

That solution—the Incarnation, life, sacrificial death, resurrection and ascension of His Son, Jesus Christ, and the establishment of the sacraments, and of His Church to dispense those sacraments and to conserve and teach the truths revealed by Him and in Him—that solution, I say, must surely affect our handling of the developmental crises of our children and the fostering of their growth into children of God.

We may recognize the psycho-dynamics involved in the process of personality growth and development, whether or not we use Freudian terms. But we cannot adopt Neo-Freudian non-intervention in that process.

We *must* use the tools given us by God, by His Son Jesus Christ, and by the Church He founded to carry on His work of salvation. That work surely devolves on parents in the first instance. The ego to be fostered and developed is that of a brother or sister of Christ our Lord, a child of God, and the superego to be guided and strengthened is an informed conscience, informed by God's laws and by the authoritative moral teachings of His Vicar on earth.

The second thing that is of extreme import is the significance of the latency period.

As I said earlier, this period or stage, while not a measure of time or age, does coincide more or less with middle childhood, i.e., the pre-pubertal years. In the words of the Group for the Advancement of Psychiatry, it is "a period of apparent quiescence or control of sexual drives occurring between early childhood and adolescence—*in which individual development and learning make great strides, and the traditional group culture comes to bear through child training and educational practices,* (emphasis added).... It is a stage characterized by a fairly stable equilibrium within a personality...a respite between the preceding stage of development and adolescence, during which the growth of the ego goes on at a great pace as it consolidates old functions and acquires new ones for coping with the drives for adapting socially and intellectually" (G.A.P. Report No. 68, 1968, pp. 756 & 790). The importance and significance of the latency period are stated in the underlined clause above.

From it two very important and practical conclusions emerge:

1. *During latency, adult communication with him about adult sex is an intrusion into an important and necessary privacy,* according to Vann Spruill, M.D., a psycho-

analyst. Therefore, no overt sex-instruction should be given either at home or in the classroom at this stage. If questions are asked by the child, either at home or in the classroom, they must be handled tactfully, prudently, truthfully, with great care, and in the classroom situation especially, very firmly, if it becomes obvious that the child asking the question is not doing so in good faith, but is intent on "showing off," or achieving status, or whatever. In the classroom, the right to privacy of the other children is to be protected.

In most cases, however, such questions are innocently put; the child is mostly seeking reassurance. These latency children assuredly do not demand a manual on "How to do it!" any more than the child who plays with matches needs a book on arson!

2. *"The child in his latency is educationally ideal"* (Melvin Anchell, M.D. *A Second Look at Sex Education,* Educulture Inc., Santa Monica, 1972). If anyone has any doubts about the importance and truth of that statement, let him simply ask himself these questions—"Why are the professional sex-educators so anxious to get their hands on our children at this stage of their development? Why do all the classroom sex-education courses promoted by SIECUS (Sex Information and Education Council of the U.S.) and AASECT (American Association of Sex Educators, Counsellors and Therapists) focus their attention on instruction in the mere mechanics of sexuality and copulation and the physical pleasure associated with it, in the 4th and 5th grades?"

Parents should realize and act on this truth, so that "The traditional group culture comes to bear" (G.A.P. Report No. 68). For us the traditional group culture in question begins with the Judaeo-Christian heritage.

Now is the time when the commandments of God, both of the Old Testament and the New, will be and must be indelibly engraved not on tablets of stone, but in the unfolding eager mind of the child and his developing superego or conscience, in his heart, in his very being. With sound reasoning, albeit the deceitful depraved wisdom of the serpent who is the enemy of God and man, the modernists seek to de-emphasize the commandments in our childrens' catechetical instruction. "They are too negative!" they cry. "The emphasis must be on love,"—especially, we note, on love of man.

All of the ten commandments are positive as well as negative in their thrust: most of them have a positive statement as well as a prohibition; some are exclusively positive precepts.

For example: the first—"I am the Lord your God: you shall not have false gods before me."

The second—"Do not take the name of God in vain." With the revelation of His goodness as well as His majesty and power in the Person and life on earth of His Son, these two could be and were combined by our Lord into the first and great commandment of the law: "You shall love the Lord your God with your whole heart and with your whole soul, and with your whole mind."

The third: "Remember to keep holy the Lord's day."

And the fourth: "Honor your father and your mother." All of these are quite evidently positive commands.

Parental example of a mutually warm, loving and non-exploitative relationship, a devout and prayerful life, attendance at Mass and reception of the sacraments, embody the fulfillment of these commandments and show the growing child what they mean in practice. But even the negatively worded commandments, the 5th

(You shall not kill) and the 7th (You shall not steal) have their positive correlative obligations:

a) To forbear with one another, curbing anger and aggressive impulses.

b) Respect for the rights and property of others.

They have, of course, also been summed up in the powerful thrust given them by our divine Lord's formulation:

"And the second is like to this: You shall love your neighbor as yourself."

How vitally important is this summing-up of all God's commands into two fundamental ones, on which "depend the whole law and the prophets" as our Lord said!

It is vital for all of us, if we are to achieve our God-given destiny; it is even more vital for our children who are in their latency period, that period "essential for developing the men and women of a higher civilization," to quote Dr. Melvin Anchell *(op. cit.)*.

He goes on later to say, "All through latency the child learns to feel love for other people. In latency, the first stirring of compassionate feeling arises from the conversion of sexual energy into affection. The affectionate love in this asexual stage is first felt for parents or for those responsible for the child's total care. Later in life, this love is also felt for other love objects."

We had better make sure we get the utmost mileage out of the latency period in the religious and moral formation of our children.

— 2 —

Jesus, the Exemplar Latency Child

In this session let us take up again the theme with which I left you in the previous lecture, namely, that it behooves us to exploit to the full the unique opportunity for religious and moral formation provided by that very important stage in personality growth and development known as the latency period.

To quote once more from Dr. Melvin Anchell's book, *A Second Look at Sex Education:* "Latency is not a hypothetical matter. No one need doubt its reality. This period has a practical application in education. The child in his latency is educationally ideal. For example, throughout the period of latency curiosity and the instinct for knowledge are derived from the redirection of childhood sexual energies."

The challenge to Catholic parents is to see to it that the redirection of energies, the curiosity and the instinct for knowledge spoken of by Dr. Anchell, are all exploited to the full in imparting to the child the truths of the Faith and the God-given rules by which he or she must live.

In a way God's dealings with the people of Israel are a prototype of the effort needed to instill in our children an awareness of the nature of God, particularly as Creator, Father and Lawgiver. In a way, too, the Israelites were like the pre-latency child, becoming aware of extrapersonal reality—other beings with whom relations existed and with whom coexistence required rules. Rules were also necessary for preservation of the identity and integrity of God's chosen people, just as they are essential for the protection of the developing ego of the child—protection from pressure of his own subconscious drives and the disruptive threat of external forces.

In the history of the chosen people, as recounted in the Old Testament, it soon became evident that rules or laws were, by themselves, not sufficient. The bonds of original sin and Evil were too strong: a Redeemer and an exemplar greater than the prophets was needed.

"And in the fullness of time God sent his only-begotten Son." The Incarnation of God the Son, the Second Person of the Blessed Trinity, was the second cataclysmic action in time of the Blessed Trinity, the first being the creation.

In relation to the latency period through which your children are now passing, the phrase "fullness of time" is very appropriate, for now is the time for them to really begin to get to know Jesus. This is the time when they begin to compete with their peers, to learn, to follow leaders.

This is the time in which they are beginning to learn skills, to develop good physical habits, work and study habits, responsible behavior, self-discipline and obedience; this, as you are aware, is the time when they are most biddable, for the most part. And this is the time when above all they need to have the model Child and Leader, Jesus, repeatedly brought to their attention.

The latency period is in a real way rather like the hidden life of Jesus, a time for learning all sorts of skills and disciplines, but above all, virtue—obedience, respect for authority, self-discipline or at least its beginnings. "And the child grew in wisdom and grace before God and men."

Jesus is unquestionably the exemplar latency child. The above statement can only have been made under the inspiration of the Holy Spirit for our guidance as to the goal we should be striving toward in the upbringing of our children—*growth in wisdom and grace*. Since in Jesus Christ, God-made-man, there was but one Person, all perfect and complete from all eternity, there can be no question of personality growth and development as we understand it and see it occurring in our children. Growing in wisdom and grace can only refer to the unfolding of His human nature which was God's most perfect creation.

But since one of the purposes of the Incarnation was to restore human nature entirely so that individual persons possessing that human nature could once again be rendered capable of sharing in the divine life, and to show us how to achieve that goal, we can infer that the above statement also refers to that particular aspect of the Incarnation—Jesus as the model of how we and our children must grow.

The only other Scriptural statement about the hidden life of Jesus is no less revealing.

"And going down to Nazareth he was subject to them." The influence of the Holy Family of Nazareth, mirrored in the Catholic home, must be paramount at all stages of our children's growth and development. It is especially vital during the latency period since most of the child's good habits must be laid down firmly during this stage.

Above all, this is the time when the child must be helped to form a correct conscience. Parents are the chief architects in this effort. We have plenty of testimony on this score from psychiatrists and psycho-analysts.

Thus Dr. Anchell: "The human conscience develops under the influence of parental leadership...without a conscience, the individual becomes a barbarian."

And Dr. Anna Freud, "Any dislocation of a child's ties with its parents may disturb its moral development and formation of character...its already extensively constructed superego...can re-oppose no real inner volition to the instinctual impulses which press for satisfaction. The origin of many anti-social and character abnormalities may be explained in this way" (Anna Freud, *The Psycho-Analytic Treatment of Children*).

Now for the Catholic the "real inner volition" that can successfully oppose the instinctual drives and.establish control is the power of grace infused into the soul at Baptism. This grace is a real sharing in the divine life, impelling the soul toward God. But the soul is imprisoned in the body as it were; and the great task of orienting all bodily activities, and indeed everything done by that complex of spirit and matter we call the human person, toward its Creator—a life-long struggle as we know—has been enormously facilitated by the Incarnation of the Son of God. For the human being, complexed as he is of spirit and body, *needed* the Incarnation, needed God-made-man, so that he could reach out and, as it were, touch God in the flesh. More than that! He can nourish his soul by partaking of the heavenly banquet provided by God's Son made man: His flesh and blood for the life of the world. "For my flesh is meat indeed, and my blood is drink indeed."

This Jesus, our Savior and Brother, is the only effective link between us and God, the only final revelation to us of God's will for man, the only One who can deliver us from the pressures of the id, those instinctual unruly passions released by original sin, and from the constant subversive efforts of Satan.

Christ alone can provide the only worthwhile motivation and sanction for virtuous living. He is the prime Model of purity, of chastity, of modesty, of obedience, of filial love, of sacrificial selfless love of others, of justice, of charity, of prudence, of meekness, of righteous indignation at wrongdoing, of courage, of dedication to duty, of humility, of genuine self-respect and self-love, of integrity, of fidelity, of how God wants us to love Him.

We must ourselves know Jesus, our Brother; we must by all means in our power, in season and out of season, strive to bring our children to know Jesus also as Brother, Exemplar and Leader. And the right time to intensify that effort and bring it to fruition is *now,* during the latency period. So much is at stake now, so much can be accomplished during this quiescent receptive period, so much can be lost!

Let us all resolve to make the most of it, to achieve the optimal religious and moral formation of our children. Let us also resolve, most firmly and passionately, not to allow anyone to usurp our prerogative and our opportunity by exposing our children to authoritative explicit instruction in the mechanics of sexual behavior at this critical stage of their personality development.

Formal sex-education courses at this stage are *virtually guaranteed* to lead to premature sexual activity. If you do not believe me, perhaps you will believe the main proponents of classroom sex-education, SIECUS, whose consultants, Dr. Joyce Ladner and Boone E. Hammond, made a similar statement: "Learning about sex at an early age indicates an increased probability that sexual activities will be engaged in early" (U.S. Dept. of

H.E.W. Report on Family Planning, 1966). More than that results, however. "The emotionless polygamy of carnally indoctrinated students becomes limitless," says Dr. Melvin Anchell, whose book, *A Second Look at Sex Education,* can be recommended strongly to your attention.

Formal sex-education at this stage is likely, however, to produce not only moral imbeciles but uneducated imbeciles as well because of interference with the normal learning process.

Let us concede that the sex-educators are *tactically* correct from their point of view in attempting to mount their programs in the elementary school grades. But let us prevent them from carrying out their plans to "turn out the correct kind of person for the new society," so far as our children are concerned. Instead, let us bend our energies and our prayers to the task of giving our children during latency the solid religious and moral formation they need to "grow in wisdom and grace before God and men."

— 3 —

The Emergence from Latency: the Work of the Holy Spirit

Throughout the latency period your child has been growing physically as well as mentally. The bodily growth, it is true, is not as striking or dramatic as it will be later on in the pubertal and post-pubertal years. But the now-known facts of biology, notably the advancing knowledge of the endocrine system, or system of glands that produce the chemical compounds known as hormones, indicate that in the pre-pubertal period from the age of eight or nine years there are progressing changes in endocrine balance that result in body sensations and emotional stirrings premonitory of the upsurge in sexual drive that occurs with puberty.

The most obvious reflection of this gradual biophysiologic buildup toward puberty is an increase in activity and energy. Now this very clearly is quite variable from one child to another: the range of normal is quite wide and there is as little need to be overly concerned with the child who remains quiet and placid as there is to attribute the increased physical activity and boisterousness, exhibited at the other extreme of normal, to a pathologic hyperkinetic syndrome, so-called, or to a character disorder.

Parents with common sense seldom have any difficulty in recognizing this range of normal—they have seen it in their own children, or others. Parenthetically this is one valuable contribution made by large families, the provision of a sufficient number of "normal" samples to be observed in more than one generation, so that the pooled observations of many individuals adds to the fund of common sense and stability of the community. In fact if the one- or two-child family were to become the norm and to be mandated for a few generations there would be a gradual and rather disastrous loss of an irreplaceable input to this pool of common sense and wisdom, and a great upsurge in parental and child anxiety neurosis. To some extent, in the so-called advanced nations this is already observable as a matter of clinical experience.

It is of some importance to recognize that bodily development and growth are occurring; it is of course more important to recognize and foster the mental and intellectual skills that are developing while the latency period provides a respite from infantile strivings and urges. But of the *utmost* importance is the religious and moral formation that are uniquely possible during this period.

The latency child still has fantasies and daydreams but is more and more capable of reality-testing and of some degree of reflective thought. He is also beginning to be capable of grasping the reality of historical events and persons.

It is at this time particularly that the child can be brought to some beginning realization of the unique historical event we know as the Incarnation, and the unique results—that Jesus lived on this earth at a given point in time, and that He still lives among us, though in a different and mysterious way.

The full import of the Incarnation of God the Son cannot be appreciated by us during this life, no matter how learned or wise we are. But your child, by now, will have gained a great deal of factual information about our Lord: the twin purposes of His coming on earth will be known—our redemption from sin and restoration to the life of supernatural grace (conferred by Baptism), and our salvation, i.e., the preservation of the supernatural life through the means provided by Him.

The child must be taught not only the lessons of the hidden life of our Lord, but the story of His public life—His teaching, His miracles, His passion, death, resurrection and ascension into heaven. He must know about the establishment by our Lord of the Church to be the safekeeper and expositor of His teaching, as well as the dispenser of the fruits of His redemption of us by means of the sacraments that He instituted.

The story of the Church, its nature and structure as well as its role, and our place in it will be grasped at least in rudimentary form by the child at this stage. The child must above all be helped to begin to know Jesus as a Person, as Savior, Lord, Brother and Model. And surely at this stage when maternal ties are secure, stable and central in the child's world, he must begin to know and love Mary as the Mother of our Lord and as our Mother also, the Mother of the Church. The child's growing ability to cope with reality, to discipline himself, to begin to acquire virtue, cannot but be helped enormously by the practice of regular personal and family prayer and the reception of the Sacraments of Penance and the Holy Eucharist. What a travesty of parental love and care it would be to be preoccupied solely with the child's physical health, well-being and comfort to the neglect of his spiritual welfare!

All the setbacks, trials and tribulations of childhood, the illnesses, the unkindness or cruelty or selfishness of others, are inevitable. They must be borne, willy-nilly. But for the child brought up in a truly Catholic home they can be given meaning and used to develop character and virtue. Without this salvific approach they can and do produce festering sores, leading to juvenile delinquents and even social psychopaths.

It is difficult indeed, for any of us to strike the proper balance between true Christian fortitude and insistence on our just and essential rights, and Christian charity and forbearance with those who injure or seek to injure us, whether in person, reputation or property. The intrinsic essential tension generated by this paradoxical seeming conflict between the imperative of standing up for what we know to be right and our Lord's instruction to turn the other cheek, to love our enemies, is inherent in the Christian condition. It is evident clearly in the public life of our Lord. It was the same Lord who forgave sinners and who drove the money-changers from the Temple with a whip made of little cords. The same Lord who said, "Be meek and humble of heart" and "Blessed are the peacemakers," also said, "I come not to bring peace but the sword." We would do well to ponder this paradox as we read or hear the words of St. Paul, "Let this mind be in you, which was also in Christ Jesus." Putting on the mind of Christ—that is the goal of Christian education.

So we must teach our children, especially at this stage of their childhood, to be manly or womanly, to stand up for what is right, but to avoid arrogance or bullying; to insist on fair treatment for all, not to be cowed or intimidated by bullies, but not to be vindictive in return; to be magnanimous in victory but not overcome by self-pity in defeat; to be able to enjoy success with true humility and to put up with failure with equanimity.

This age when the child is beginning to feel the first faint stirrings of biological manhood or womanhood can be a difficult time. It is a time when any setbacks or failures, apparent or real, can be very discouraging and can lead to regressive behavior. For example, a minor injury, especially if incurred under what he considers unfair conditions, may evoke tears in a boy who hitherto would have taken such an event in his stride; the prepubertal girl under similar circumstances may react by returning to playthings or clothes from an earlier age. Both may seek to retreat into the protected cocoon of the home from the hurly-burly of peer conflict, like the Apostles in the days and weeks preceding Pentecost. One must be aware of such tendencies and occurrences and the reason for them. Sympathy must be tempered with firm encouragement to rejoin the fray.

And just as the infant Church, in the persons of the Blessed Virgin Mary, the Apostles and disciples, had its faith and supernatural life confirmed and indeed set ablaze by the power of the Holy Spirit on Pentecost Sunday, so too your child will be confirmed. The Sacrament of Confirmation will reaffirm his adoption as a son of God in Baptism, and strengthen the life of grace in his soul by the gifts of the Holy Spirit.

Why do we not seem to recognize the reality of the tremendous and profound impact this sacrament must have, this final formal ratification, by sacramental rite of the Church, of the indwelling of the Blessed Trinity in the soul? It cannot but affect the maturation—psycho-sexual, characterological, behavioral—of your latency child in his pre-pubertal years. Problems of adjustment, behavioral problems, peer rivalry and conflict there may be, there will be, but unless they stem from organic nervous or mental diseases, their resolution can be influenced and their ego-strengthening potential will be aided by the sacramental life of the confirmed Catholic.

In truth, successful emergence from latency and successful navigation of the frequently stormy waters of adolescence is the work of the Holy Spirit.

PART THREE

Post-Latency Children

— 1 —
God's Plan: Creation and Pro-Creation

In earlier lectures it was stated that the terms *pre-latency*, *latency*, and *post-latency* referred to stages of psycho-sexual development, so-called, and that strictly speaking they were not measures of chronological age, though they did correspond more or less with rather loosely-delimited chronological and biological periods in the life and development of the child. Thus children till about age six, seven, or eight years are usually pre-latency; from age seven or eight till eleven, twelve or thirteen, they are in the latency period; and from eleven, twelve or thirteen they are post-latency (pubertal and adolescent). We need to define what is meant by *pubertal* and *adolescent*, though I am sure all of you have a more or less accurate and adequate notion of what the terms mean.

"Pubertal" refers of course to puberty. The Group for the Advancement of Psychiatry states that puberty is primarily a biological, maturational, hormonal and growth process, whereas adolescence is a psychological, social and maturational process initiated by puberty. We can also accept their statement that adolescence is a developmental phenomenon unique to man, since this is no more than a matter of common observation.

Their account of the complex biological changes associated with puberty, the hormonal changes leading to increased and differential growth, gonadal maturation, development of external genitalia and secondary sex characteristics—the essential anatomical and physiological changes confronting the growing individual—this account is accurate and succinct.

So also is the account given of different patterns of adolescence and adolescent-adult relationships in different societies and cultures—a sort of sociological-anthropological survey which is naturally non-judgmental. There is one obvious and glaring exception: nowhere is there any observation on adolescence in a truly Christian or Catholic culture. This is of course for us a great deficit; as a result much of what they have to say and conclude about "normality" in adolescence is simply irrelevant for the Catholic, and indeed if taken seriously could lead us astray.

We can, however, concede two of the main theses they put forward:

1. From the beginning of recorded history, references to youth indicate that adults characteristically view adolescents with considerable ambivalence. Thus Hesiod, one of the Fathers of Greek literature, wrote in the 8th century B.C.:

> "I see no hope for the future of our people if they are dependent on the frivolous youth of today, for certainly all youth are reckless beyond words.... When I was a boy, we were taught to be discreet and respectful of elders...."

It has a modern ring, does it not? And the Roman poet Horace gives a matchless description of the old man—"querulous, ornery, always harping on how things were when he was a boy, critical and censorious of the young."

Which of us has not at one time or another relived this experience? "And today's adolescents, from their position as the new adult generation, will express the same kinds of concerns about adolescents as were only recently expressed about them" (G.A.P. Report No. 68).

2. "Though adolescence is usually a troubled and stressful time of life characterized by questioning and rebelling against the rules and values of their parents and/or society, it does not follow that nothing can be done to alleviate the conflict. For adolescence must be seen as a constructive stage in human development, both for the individual adolescent and for society" (G.A.P. Report No. 68).

To this we can say a hearty *Amen!*

Where we part company from our colleagues of The Group for the Advancement of Psychiatry is on the subject of what is necessary to aid the often difficult passage from childhood through adolescence to adulthood.

For the approach of G.A.P. is the traditional psychoanalytic one, i.e., elucidation and understanding the psychodynamics of the process will not only illuminate the transition, but facilitate it and increase the understanding and rapport between the adolescent and adult generations. It is essentially a secular and humanist approach, and while we can agree that knowing the biological and psycho-dynamic facts of the problem helps us understand and sympathize with our children's developmental growing pains, we simply cannot abandon them to what an older generation of physicians called *vis medicatrix naturae*—the healing power of nature. We must help them as well as try to understand them.

Understanding them means not only realizing the stage of biological and physical stresses they are passing through, with its corresponding reawakening of primal urges that sometimes bid fair to overwhelm the developing ego, but also remembering the level of supernatural life at which the struggle for mastery is joined.

It seems providential that according to local Church discipline some children enter this stage of their development as confirmed Christians, having received the Sacrament of Confirmation. For, as stated already, it is a stage of profound bodily change, of emerging physical maturity, coinciding not only with the re-emergence of strong sexual interests and drives under the hormonal influence of puberty, but also with the painful struggle to survive adolescence—the conflict between the almost arrogant need to be independent and the subconscious realization of dependence, feelings of utter inadequacy and worthlessness alternating with surges of boundless self-confidence, competence and energy, of feeling able to do everything, and yet able to do nothing right. The adolescent's conviction that nobody can understand him or what he is experiencing, least of all his parents, has some basis in fact.

Though all of us have passed safely and successfully through puberty and adolescence, our recollection of that experience can aid us only to achieve sympathy with but not complete understanding of the problems of *this* adolescent son or daughter.

For we are finite individual beings, and for each of us the experience of life is a unique experience, despite common denominators, similarities of circumstance, and coincidences sometimes quite striking.

But Christianity and the supernatural life of grace add an entirely new dimension to human life, and each of its stages. God the Father, Son and Holy Spirit *do* understand each one of us individually and completely, and to each divine Person can be attributed a salvific role in the successful passage to maturity and adulthood. This time of puberty, then, is a time for renewed and more detailed instruction in the divine plan of Creation and pro-creation, a time for prudent and individualized instruction in the essential biological "facts of life" and their relation to the divine plan. This instruction will of course have a somewhat different slant and emphasis in boys than in girls, though a common ground of knowledge of the unique difference in structure, function and role of the opposite sex is self-evident.

Pope John Paul II presented a series of analytic and didactic reflections on the Book of Genesis accounts of the creation of man at his weekly general audiences from September 5, 1979 to April 2, 1980. They provided a remarkable survey of authentic biblical anthropology as revealed in the simple but profound language of the written Word. From its analysis he developed insights into the state in which man was created "in the beginning," his uniqueness (one of the meanings of his "original solitude"), his nature ("male and female he created them"), his corporality and original innocence, his personhood, the nuptial meaning of the body, and indeed the elements of a complete theology of the body and of marriage. Nothing quite comparable has emanated from the Holy See. The series has been published (see reading list); it requires careful reading and reflection and together with the recent papal Apostolic Exhortation on the Family it provides essential background for the kind of parental instruction of adolescents to which reference is made in the preceding paragraph.

How and when it will be given will vary from family to family and within families. Some children can readily be given verbal instruction, others cannot—they "know it all" (from their peers), and will not ask questions nor listen to any answers, but most will read a booklet if urged to do so. An excellent series very suitable for the purpose is available. (See reading list.)

They will undoubtedly be learning the biological facts of reproduction, plant and animal, in science classes in school; one must make sure, by whatever means—scrutiny of texts, judicious questioning of the child, etc.—that they have the proper information and that they understand it within the limits of their ability and level of educational achievement. Misinformation they will get, from their peers, and because of the intrinsic difficulty of transferring what is read or heard to personal experience. It takes patient effort to correct such misinformation, and not infrequently the effort may not bear fruit until the adolescent begins to be able to reassert himself against the drives of the id for mastery.

But mostly our children need *reassurance* about it all. They should have had some preparatory explanations of what occurs at puberty—the bodily maturation, the physical consequences, for example, menstruation and nocturnal seminal emission, and be assured of the normality of these events. And above all else, they need reassurance of the goodness of God, His Fatherhood, His creative power, the role He intended for this mysterious disturbing powerful appetite that is awakening, the unruly nature of this drive because of the effects of original sin, and the enormous help He has provided for its control in the power of prayer and the sacraments.

Always the goal of our efforts is formation, even when imparting information—formation of healthy habits of self-control in regard to other appetites, e.g., food, candies, other luxuries; attitudes of respect and reverence for the bodies and the physical powers given us by God, reverence especially for those bodies as the temples of the Holy Spirit, the dwelling places of the Blessed Trinity. Understanding of the function of pleasure, and of pain and suffering in God's plan for us, must be made an integral part of the intellectual, moral and spiritual equipment of the adolescent so that *a habitual inclination to the proper use of creatures* will grow as he grows. It is not easy for any of us, least of all in our adolescence, to learn to walk this straight and narrow path that leads to salvation.

But our Father in heaven did not leave us to our own devices in our attempts to do His will. He has, in His infinite love and mercy, provided us with totally undeserved and totally effective means to walk that road and to achieve our destination. In the next two lectures of this series we will discuss with you those means and how we should use them.

— 2 —
Jesus, the Way, the Truth and the Life

The first indispensable means given us by Almighty God whereby we may grow in His love and grace and achieve our eternal destiny is His own Beloved Son, our Lord and Savior, Jesus Christ. "For there is no other name, under heaven, given to men by which they may be saved," said St. Paul. Jesus, in His life on earth, His teachings and His actions, provides the only possible blueprint for the Christian life. In His Person He is the final perfect Revelation of God, and of God's divine plan for mankind, for you and for me, and for our children.

The latter, at this stage of their growth and development, are in dire need of the saving grace and divine power that entered into human history with the Incarnation of the Son of God, never to leave it. Henceforth, things would never be the same: since then, men could never again say God was a distant mysterious Being—ineffable, unknowable. When the Apostle Philip said, "Lord, show us the Father and it will be sufficient for us," our Lord's reply rings out to us also, "Philip, he who sees me, sees also the Father."

To see Jesus, to know Him more intimately than we know our relatives or friends, and in Him to know the Godhead Incarnate—that is the goal toward which we all strive, that is what life is all about, not bodily health nor well-being (though these we cherish as gifts of God), not material nor professional success (though bound we are to make good and profitable use of the talents God has given to us). Rather, "let this mind be in you which was also in Christ Jesus," as St. Paul urges.

Insofar as we approach this goal, thus far do we become mature persons, Christian persons. Insofar as we fall short of it we remain immature, petty, half-baked, nonentities, regardless of our worldly success or achievement.

Our divine Lord came on earth as He Himself told us "not to destroy the law but to fulfill it."

And so He reiterated and amplified the teachings of the old law and the prophets, including the ten commandments. To be sure He expanded on the latter—"You have heard that it was said to them of old: You shall not kill.... But I say to you, that whosoever is angry with his brother shall be in danger of the judgment." This and the entire Sermon on the Mount is but the first overt development of doctrine recorded by the Evangelist.

But He also put the law and the prophets in proper perspective. "On these two commandments depend the whole law and the prophets," He said after He had replied to the question, "Master, which is the great commandment in the law?" And what are these two commandments? The first and greatest according to Jesus is "You shall love the Lord your God with your whole heart, and with your whole soul, and with your whole mind." And the second is like to this: "You shall love your neighbor as yourself."

Why is it like to the first? Because by His Incarnation Jesus took the first step in restoring humanity to something like its primal position; "Let us make man to our own image and likeness," said the three divine Persons in the creative act. That image was tarnished by original sin, but already in God's plan it was restored to its pristine beauty in the Immaculate Conception of the Mother of His Son, and soon was to be offered anew to all human beings, purified and cleansed by the Sacrifice of the cross.

Henceforth, "as long as you did it to the least of these my brethren you did it to me."

Jesus restored man completely—not just his spirit, but the whole person, his whole being. Henceforth all man's actions, all his appetites, including his sexual urges, must be oriented toward the more perfect realization of God's plan for man.

Henceforth, the sixth and ninth commandments take on a new force, a positive force stemming from love of God, love of self and love of neighbor.

These are the only sanctions adequate for the strong prohibitions, so counter to man's fallen nature, of the sixth and ninth commandments—"You shall not commit adultery," "You shall not covet your neighbor's wife." These had already been amplified by our Lord Himself to include lustful thoughts and desires as well as acts.

The Holy Father, Pope John Paul II, followed up his series of catechetical general audience addresses on the book of Genesis with yet another. These reflections were on particular statements of our Lord in His Sermon on the Mount and on related doctrinal statements in the letters of St. Paul. From them the Pope developed the essentials of the authentic Christian theology of the body and provided a powerful catechesis on marriage and the virtue of chastity. They should be read and studied by parents, teachers and indeed all Christian men and women including your older and more mature children. They are essential background reading for the simple summary exposition of traditional Catholic teaching that follows. This traditional teaching was developed from the beginning of the Christian Way, and we need to remind ourselves that it was developed and took root and flourished in a pagan civilization that was as corrupt and debauched, from the moral point of view, as our own. From the beginning it was based solidly on the teachings of the Lord and in particular those related to the difficult but absolutely essential virtue of chastity. This virtue we must emphasize right away is necessary for all—for the married couple, the unmarried laity, no less than for the celibate priest, religious sister or brother. It must be taught by word and by example. The witness of chaste parents, and of chaste celibate priests, religious and lay persons is a powerful and indispensable buttress to the authentic authoritative teachings of the Church. The latter, we repeat, is always referred back to Christ the Lord.

In His own life, and in that of His Blessed Mother and foster father, St. Joseph, Jesus gives us the example we need to live out our lives in purity of mind and heart, and in chastity. These twin virtues, purity and chastity, and their handmaiden modesty, are virtues that must be developed in our children, when with the bodily changes of puberty, they are inevitably going to have to contend with the sexual appetite, "the law of the flesh striving against the law of the spirit," as St. Paul so aptly puts it.

Let us soberly reflect for a while on the implications of all that we know about human sexuality and the attitudes and convictions we must strive to develop about it in our post-latency children. We know very well that it was and is a part of God's plan for mankind, therefore good. We know also that for human beings this is no simple biological urge geared only to reproduction of the species, but of its very nature, because of man's nature, it has a uniquely unitive, creative and pro-creative purpose. We know its unitive power does not long survive willful deliberate suppression of its pro-creative purpose, but *can* survive involuntary barrenness, as witness the number of stable non-fertile marriages. In ordinary circumstances, it is possible for a couple to be pro-creative without being united in the marriage bond; a married couple *can* be united even if for them, through no fault of theirs, sexual union is non-productive of offspring. Their bond will be *creative* of family, even if not pro-creative, for they will frequently seek to adopt a child or even several children. But if sexual union is habitually and deliberately divorced from its pro-creative purpose it will prove neither unitive nor creative. We also know that this powerful appetite became unruly as one of the results of original sin, and that it can easily get out of control as the other instinctual drives also can, unless we learn self-discipline, and enlist the power of self-denial, prayer and the sacraments.

We must also know that while sexuality is important, it is not all important, and that it is a lie to say that unless one is sexually active one is not normal.

There is really no excuse for believing Catholics who accept or seem to accept that untruth, propagated by the father of lies. We *know* that marital and extra-marital chastity are possible, that celibacy is possible. We know that in the Roman Catholic Church countless generations of priests and religious have given witness to that fact, that many lay people also, who have chosen to remain single or who in God's Providence have not found a spouse, have been able to remain continent and chaste with the help of His grace.

We know more than that. We have our Lord's own testimony that not all are called to the married state and that the state of consecrated virginity is the highest of all callings to which a man or woman may aspire. We will deal with this matter more fully in the third and final lecture of this series.

Suffice it to say now that apart from reassuring our post-latency, post-pubertal adolescent children that the involuntary physical phenomena and pleasurable sensations associated with the biological sexual drive are in themselves good and ordained by God for a very special purpose, they must be led to the conviction that such a pleasurable good must be reserved for the purpose for which it was created.

Here is where the Catholic must part company, decisively, from the amoral, non-judgmental, psychoanalytic, psycho-therapeutic, neo-Freudian school of thought.

For some of them, psycho-sexual maturation means liberation from any pangs of conscience or guilt feelings about sexual sinning, whether the sinning be heterosexual, homosexual, or perverse.

It is difficult to understand how so many people have been duped by such an absurd proposition. If the theorists were to proclaim as the goal of psychotherapy for sociopaths such as kleptomaniacs, arsonists or murderers, the achievement of freedom from "hang-ups" of guilt and shame while they continued to indulge their "appetites," they would be laughed to scorn or hounded from practice.

Anna Freud was nearer to the Christian viewpoint when she wrote: "Shame and disgust are important in restraining the child's anal and exhibitionistic impulses from breaking through to gratification" *(The Psycho-Analytical Treatment of Children)*. But sexual urges are not the only narcissistic tendencies our adolescent children have to contend with. Their preoccupation with their own private concerns, appearance, acceptance or rejection by peer groups, real or imagined; their ambivalence toward parents and parental values; their sometimes fierce drives toward independence and cutting adrift from the home alternating with almost regressive dependency—all these phenomena must be dealt with sympathetically but firmly. Our children must be brought to see that they are but temptations in the literal sense of that word, i.e., trials of their character, personality and virtue. They are temporary, and are to be used constructively toward the goal of achieving the only kind of "identity," of ego strength, that fits a man or woman for this life or for eternal life—the goal of sanctity. Parental patience, understanding and example are the primary tools for helping our children through this period.

But for us and for our children the prime exemplars are our Divine Lord, His Blessed Mother, and Saint Joseph.

Nor can we forget the Mystical Body of Christ, the communion of saints, those countless men and women whose lives prove to us that "My yoke indeed is sweet and my burden light."

Stories and lives of the saints should have been a constant part of our children's reading and listening fare from their early childhood. Not infrequently they can be helped over some of the difficult hurdles of adolescence by a revival or renewal of interest in the achievements of one or other of those exemplary heroes of the spiritual life.

It is scarcely possible to exaggerate the power for good of good books, or the corrupting influence of bad books. The same holds for the new non-printed media.

Good books and films are more than ever essential to intellectual and moral health in the modern age. Contemporary literature, entertainment and the media, especially television, all conspire to produce a distorted neo-pagan vision of man, his origin, his destiny and his values. Few movies and television programs nowadays depict normal healthy attitudes and family relationships. Rather they portray love as existing mostly outside of marriage and the family. Sex is for fun; responsibility, concern for others are out of date; self-fulfillment, self-gratification and feeling good are the norms for ethical behavior. Adolescents must be helped to be discriminating and critical of what they view on the screen, and efforts must continue by all means to reform and purify the mass media and to provide wholesome alternative programs. The home and the school must collaborate closely in educating children, especially adolescents, to be equally discriminating in what they read.

There is no single book or short book-list that will prove helpful to every adolescent. What we need to insure is that in the home a wide variety is available to our children and that both by precept and by example we have already imbued them with a love of good books and of reading.

Meantime, to those who say, "But books are outmoded," we can only reply with Lord Goodman, "They speak not for man, but for the apes."

— 3 —
The Holy Spirit, the Sanctifier

In this final lecture of the series, we take up again the topic of sanctity, of holiness. What is this thing, this entity which we call holiness? In the practical sphere it is nothing less than a complete identification with the will of God; essentially it springs from union with God, insofar as this is attainable by finite beings during their mortal existence. How do we know the will of God for us?

We know it because He has revealed it to us—in the Scriptures (the written revelation), in the life, death and resurrection of His Son, in the teachings of the Church conserving, interpreting and promulgating the body of truths to be believed and acted on, derived from the sources of written revelation and her own venerable tradition.

We know that outside the Church there is no salvation, but we also know, each of us, good and holy non-Catholics and non-Christians. We have no difficulty reconciling these two facts, because we know and have been taught that these holy ones who are not professing Christians, belong to the Church "in spirit," because God has offered and offers to all men the fruits of the redemptive sacrifice of His beloved Son, though for reasons known only to Him not all receive the complete gift of faith.

This belief of ours is a compelling one, "For this is the will of God, your sanctification."

Rather than puzzle further over this seeming paradox of our Faith, let us instead dwell on the paramount fact—the extraordinary fact of God's extreme goodness and generosity in giving to us Catholics such a marvelous headstart toward holiness. The thought ought keep us forever humble! For as we have considered with you in previous lectures, by Baptism an entirely new order of life was initiated—the supernatural life, initiated by an infusion of what the Church has called, from time immemorial, sanctifying grace, and which means a real sharing in the divine life of the Blessed Trinity. We have seen too that by the Sacrament of Confirmation, by the power of the Third Person of the Blessed Trinity, the Holy Spirit, our pre-teen children have had another formal and special infusion of sanctifying grace, a ratification of the indwelling of the Blessed Trinity in their souls.

In this discourse to the Apostles after the Last Supper, our divine Lord spelled this out very clearly: "If any one love me, he will keep my word, and my Father will love him, and we will come to him, and will make our abode with him.... But the Paraclete, the Holy Spirit whom the Father will send in my name, he will teach you all things, and bring all things to your mind, whatsoever I shall have said to you" (John 14:23, 26).

And Peter, the rock on which He founded His Church, in his inimitable, blunt and plain-spoken fashion, drew the practical and logical conclusion in his first epistle, which could be called the first papal encyclical:

"Wherefore, having the loins of your mind girt up, being sober, trust perfectly in the grace which is offered you in the revelation of Jesus Christ: As children of obedience, not fashioned according to the earlier desires of your ignorance; but according to him who has called you, who is holy, be you also in your whole conduct holy; because it is written: 'You shall be holy, for I am holy' " (1 Peter 1:13-16). What a wonderful summary of what we should be doing, and have been in these lectures trying to formulate, in regard to the education and the religious and moral formation of our children!

"Having the loins of your mind girt up": If we have given our children all that we alone can give them, and are bound to give them—a stable, holy home environment; a good Catholic school where, in addition to acquiring the secular basic educational skills, they are instructed thoroughly in the truths of the Faith, where the optimal learning time of the latency period is not pre-empted by formal sex instruction—they cannot but have "the loins of the mind girt up."

"Being sober": Rather than being indoctrinated in the ways in which man can degrade himself by sin, by means of so-called education programs in drug-abuse and human sexual abuses, they will have acquired good physical habits, be on the way to acquiring self-discipline and self-control, and begin to learn the proper use of the good things God has provided for us, the proper use of creatures.

"Trust perfectly in the grace which is offered you in the revelation of Jesus Christ": What is this grace but the inexhaustible treasure house of the Church, to which our attention and that of our children must be drawn again and again? There is the liturgy, Holy Mass—the living re-enactment, though now unbloody, of our Lord's sacrifice of the cross; the Sacraments of Penance and the Holy Eucharist, so vital to young people in their adolescent years; the Sacrament of the sick and dying; the power of personal prayer, especially the rosary; indulgences; the sacramentals; spiritual reading, especially the Scriptures.

"As children of obedience, not fashioned according to the earlier desires of your ignorance"; those "earlier desires" are surely none other than the primal urges of the Freudian "id" struggling for expression and mastery over the fragile ego. But as we have seen, we and our children are not and have never been naked Freudian egos. Our personalities, our very nature, have been transformed and energized by the infusion of supernatural sanctifying grace at Baptism, re-charged as it were by Confirmation, and nourished by the very Body and Blood of Christ and by the saving graces of the Sacrament of Penance. Though we know our struggle for mastery is not only against the unruly passions of the "id" but against the powers of darkness, the spirits of wickedness, we also know *the battle is biased in our favor*. We grew, and our children are growing, as "children of obedience" to the manifest will of our heavenly Father.

"According to him who has called you, who is holy, be you also in your whole conduct holy."

There you have it in a nutshell! The *primary vocation* of each and every one of us, and of our children, is to holiness. Their daily lives, as ours, must be touched and transformed by those powerhouses of grace we have referred to above for they are the tools of the Holy Spirit, the Sanctifier.

Give them these things and they will profit from even a mediocre secular education; without these things the finest secular education will bring them only material success.

Each and every person is called to holiness: But there is a *secondary vocation* for each as well. For each person is called to holiness in one of three states in life. They are:

1. The married state.
2. The celibate state as a priest or religious.
3. The celibate state as a single lay person.

These are the *only* states in life, "lifestyles" if you will, compatible with the holiness demanded of us by God.

Each state has its own grace of state, a special help from God to enable us to achieve holiness in that state.

In two of them a sacrament was instituted by Christ to confer that special grace of state: they are the Sacraments of *Matrimony* and *Holy Orders*.

The extent of instruction concerning these sacraments will vary from adolescent to adolescent; all need at least some instruction. Much of it can be and should be informal; already, in the sound Catholic home, the children will have assimilated, largely by non-verbal communication and the good example of their parents, a great deal of the most essential information and attitude formation concerning the married state. All that remains necessary is some degree of formal instruction on the divine origin, the sacramental nature and the teachings of the Church on Matrimony. Far too many pre-Cana and Cana conferences have been secularized—degraded to indoctrination in the anti-life contraceptive mentality and crash-courses in the techniques of avoiding the procreative responsibilities of Matrimony, while exalting the hedonistic, mutually self-satisfying aspects of married life. No mention of the saving virtue of conjugal chastity, but much ado about mutual gratification, self-indulgence and mutual understanding and fulfillment—reinforced by the most stupid, provocative and frequently dangerous sensitivity training techniques. No wonder marital unhappiness, infidelity, divorce, and all its sordid and tragic consequences are so much on the increase in the so-called advanced countries!

We *must* provide the antidote to all this poison in the wellspring of society, the family. That antidote is none other than the magisterial teachings of the Church.

Of these teachings two documents stand out in modern times: they are the Encyclicals *Casti connubii* of Pope Pius XI, and *Humanae vitae* of Pope Paul VI. In these two is to be found all you ever wanted or needed to know about sexuality and the state of matrimony! There are many excellent commentaries on the teachings of these encyclicals; the former are of educational and apologetic value. The encyclicals themselves are essential reading.

At this point a comment is in order on what has come to be known as natural family planning. In the Encyclical *Humanae vitae,* Pope Paul VI referred to responsible parenthood. He was careful to point out that "in relation to physical, economic, psychological and social conditions, responsible parenthood is exercised, *either by the deliberate and generous decision to raise a numerous family,* or by the decision, *made for grave motives and with due respect for the moral law, to avoid for the time being, or even for an indeterminate period, a new birth.*"

It is obvious that in secular humanist understanding, responsible parenthood is equated only with limitation or avoidance of births, zero population or negative population growth, by any or all means, including abortion. In this view none of such means can be immoral; the only immorality is to contribute to the so-called population explosion.

But the Pope, reiterating as he said the constant and coherent teaching of the Church, affirmed, "If there are *serious* motives to space out births, which derive from the physical or psychological conditions of husband and wife, or from external conditions,...it is then licit to take into account the natural rhythms immanent in the generative functions, for the use of marriage in the infertile periods only, and in this way to regulate births without offending the moral principles which have been recalled earlier."

Clearly the Pope was referring to natural family planning, and later in the encyclical he encouraged men of science "to explain more thoroughly the various conditions favoring a *proper* regulation of births," recalling Pope Pius XII's similar wish "that medical science succeed in providing a sufficiently secure basis for a regulation of births founded on the observance of natural rhythms."

The advances hoped for by both Pontiffs have taken place; and natural family planning using methodical observation of symptoms and/or signs identifying the time and occurrence of ovulation in the female spouse, is highly reliable, as effective as artificial contraception and accepted by more and more couples, the more the medical hazards of the major artificial methods become known to them.

It must be taught, however, only in the context of the Church's integral teaching on marriage and responsible parenthood, otherwise it can be and is abused, and can lead to an anti-life selfish mentality just as easily as artificial contraception does. *It should not be taught to adolescents.* It suffices to inform them that such reliable and morally acceptable methods of regulating fertility and conception exist and will be taught when the time comes for marriage-preparation courses.

As for those children of ours who may already be developing at least the faint beginnings of an awareness of a vocation to the priestly or religious life, they must be helped to see it against the background of three essential "givens":

1. The univocal call of God of all men to holiness.
2. The necessary role of chastity in following that call.
3. God has an individualized plan for every person.

The family, now as always, has to be the seed-bed of vocations to the priestly and religious life. However, the example and acquaintance of good and holy priests and religious in developing and fostering such vocations cannot be overemphasized. The present time has seen vocations dwindling and we are saddened by the scandal of dissenting and defecting priests and religious. All the more important is the role of good Catholic parents such as yourselves in recognizing the possibility and the beginning of a priestly or religious vocation in one of your children. We must seek out at all costs good and holy priests and religious, wherever they may be, as counselors and role-models for our children. We must be able to help our children, troubled perhaps by clerical defections and bad example, realize that such phenomena have the same origin as the ever-increasing divorce and broken home statistics, namely a failure to cultivate the virtues of chastity and fidelity, frequently due to or else leading to a loss of the Faith itself. Those three "givens" mentioned above are essential considerations for all adolescents in dealing with their possible choice of a particular state in life, their secondary vocation, whether it be a priestly or religious vocation, the married state, or the celibate single state as a lay person.

The family life we have provided them up to now and are continuing to provide, as well as the sound religious and moral formation entailed, will ensure that they scrutinize their talents and tastes carefully, prayerfully seek guidance from God through us their parents and through wise and prudent counselors, so that they may ascertain with reasonable certainty the state in life to which God is calling them. If this is not the priestly or religious life, they must be helped to choose the educational experiences both general and specialized (e.g., professional) that are most apt to equip them for optimal living in that state to which they are called.

This choice of educational preparation is part of what can be regarded as the *tertiary vocation* each person has—to the learned professions so-called, to business, to politics, to the arts and crafts, to farming, to productive labor, to the service industries. Our children must be imbued with the philosophy of the essential dignity of all honest work and with the conviction that it does not matter too much what kind of job or employment one undertakes, provided it is an honest and law-abiding occupation, that what really matters is that primary vocation to holiness, namely a life of love and service of God and fellowman, and a life of eternal happiness after death, the call to become saints. Let the Angelic Doctor have the last word: "How does one become a saint?" he was asked. St. Thomas replied, "You *will* it."

Reading List

1. Danielou, Jean Cardinal.
   God's Life in Us. Dimension Books, Denville, New Jersey, 1969.

2. Dobson, James.
   Dare to Discipline. Tyndal House Publishers, Wheaton, Illinois, 1970.

3. Dubay, Thomas.
   God Dwells Within Us. Dimension Books, Denville, New Jersey, 1970.

4. Hemingway, Leslie. *
   The Modern World and Self-Control. Polding Press, Melbourne, Australia, 1969.

5. Kelly, George A., ed.
   Human Sexuality in Our Time: What the Church Teaches. St. Paul Editions, Boston, Mass., 1979.

6. Pickering, Aidan. **
   Sex Instruction in the Home. London, England, Catholic Truth Society, 1973.

7. *Polding Press Youth Series.* **
   Polding Press, Melbourne, Australia.

8. Pope John Paul II.
   Original Unity of Man and Woman (Catechesis on the Book of Genesis). St. Paul Editions, Boston, Mass., 1981.

9. Pope John Paul II.
   "Blessed Are the Pure of Heart" (Catechesis on the Ser-

mon on the Mount and the Letters of St. Paul). St. Paul Editions, Boston, Mass., 1982.

10. Pope John Paul II.
Apostolic Exhortation on the Family *(Familiaris consortio)*. St. Paul Editions, Boston, Mass., 1982.

11. Pope Paul VI.
Encyclical *Humanae vitae*. 1968.

12. Vitz, Paul C.
Psychology as Religion: The Cult of Self-Worship. Wm. B. Eerdmans Publ. Co., 1981.

13. Von Hildebrand, D.
The Encyclical Humanae Vitae: A Sign of Contradiction. Franciscan Herald Press, Chicago, 1969.

14. Von Hildebrand, D. ***
In Defense of Purity. Franciscan Herald Press, Chicago, 1970.

15. Von Hildebrand, D.
Celibacy and the Crisis of Faith. Franciscan Herald Press, Chicago, 1971.

16. Wojtyla, Karol Cardinal.
Love and Responsibility. Farrar, Strauss and Giroux, 1981.

FOOTNOTES

* Excellent for the older adolescent.

** Two of the Polding Press Series, "Instruction for Boys," and "Instruction for Girls," may be given to 12 to 16 year olds to read. The C.T.S. pamphlet has separate talks for boys and girls; suitable for pubertal or immediately pre-pubertal children, if parents consider them ready.

*** Strongly recommended for the older adolescent and college student.

Daughters of St. Paul

IN MASSACHUSETTS
50 St. Paul's Ave., Jamaica Plain, Boston, MA 02130; **617-522-8911; 617-522-0875**
172 Tremont Street, Boston, MA 02111; **617-426-5464; 617-426-4230**
IN NEW YORK
78 Fort Place, Staten Island, NY 10301; **212-447-5071**
59 East 43rd Street, New York, NY 10017; **212-986-7580**
625 East 187th Street, Bronx, NY 10458; **212-584-0440**
525 Main Street, Buffalo, NY 14203; **716-847-6044**
IN NEW JERSEY
Hudson Mall — Route 440 and Communipaw Ave., Jersey City, NJ 07304; **201-433-7740**
IN CONNECTICUT
202 Fairfield Ave., Bridgeport, CT 06604; **203-335-9913**
IN OHIO
2105 Ontario St. (at Prospect Ave.), Cleveland, OH 44115; **216-621-9427**
25 E. Eighth Street, Cincinnati, OH 45202; **513-721-4838**
IN PENNSYLVANIA
1719 Chestnut Street, Philadelphia, PA 19103; **215-568-2638**
IN VIRGINIA
1025 King St., Alexandria, VA 22314 **703-683-1741**
IN FLORIDA
2700 Biscayne Blvd., Miami, FL 33137; **305-573-1618**
IN LOUISIANA
4403 Veterans Memorial Blvd., Metairie, LA 70002; **504-887-7631; 504-887-0113**
1800 South Acadian Thruway, P.O. Box 2028, Baton Rouge, LA 70821 **504-343-4057; 504-343-3814**
IN MISSOURI
1001 Pine Street (at North 10th), St. Louis, MO 63101; **314-621-0346; 314-231-1034**
IN ILLINOIS
172 North Michigan Ave., Chicago, IL 60601; **312-346-4228 312-346-3240**
IN TEXAS
114 Main Plaza, San Antonio, TX 78205; **512-224-8101**
IN CALIFORNIA
1570 Fifth Avenue, San Diego, CA 92101; **714-232-1442**
46 Geary Street, San Francisco, CA 94108; **415-781-5180**
IN HAWAII
1143 Bishop Street, Honolulu, HI 96813; **808-521-2731**
IN ALASKA
750 West 5th Avenue, Anchorage AK 99501; **907-272-8183**

IN CANADA
3022 Dufferin Street, Toronto 395, Ontario, Canada
IN ENGLAND
128, Notting Hill Gate, London W11 3QG, England
133 Corporation Street, Birmingham B4 6PH, England
5A-7 Royal Exchange Square, Glasgow G1 3AH, England
82 Bold Street, Liverpool L1 4HR, England
IN AUSTRALIA
58 Abbotsford Rd., Homebush, N.S.W., Sydney 2140, Australia